For my big children – D.M.
For my even bigger children – A.S.

First published in the United States 1995
by Dial Books for Young Readers
A Division of Penguin Books USA Inc.
375 Hudson Street, New York, New York 10014

Published in Great Britain by
Frances Lincoln Limited

Printed in Italy
First Edition
1 3 5 7 9 10 8 6 4 2

Library of Congress Cataloging in Publication Data
MacKinnon, Debbie.
What size? / Debbie MacKinnon; photographs by Anthea Sieveking.—1st ed.
p.   cm.
ISBN 0-8037-1745-8
1. Size perception—Juvenile literature. 2. Size judgment—Juvenile literature.
I. Sieveking, Anthea. II. Title.
BF299.S5M33   1995   153.7'52—dc20   93-40103   CIP   AC

WHAT SIZE?

Debbie MacKinnon
Photographs by Anthea Sieveking

Dial Books for Young Readers New York

Georgia and Josh are playing with cars. Josh is in the biggest car.

Big and Little

Which car is the littlest?

Ezra and Kelly are playing dress-up. Kelly's dress is the longest.

Long and Short

Which dress is the shortest?

Taran is making Play-Doh shapes.
He has rolled the pink the thinnest.

Thick and Thin

Which shape is the thickest?

Sarah, Kezia, and Dolly are sitting in chairs. Sarah's chair is the lowest.

High and Low

Which chair is the highest?

Alex is painting lines. He is finishing the widest line.

Wide and Narrow

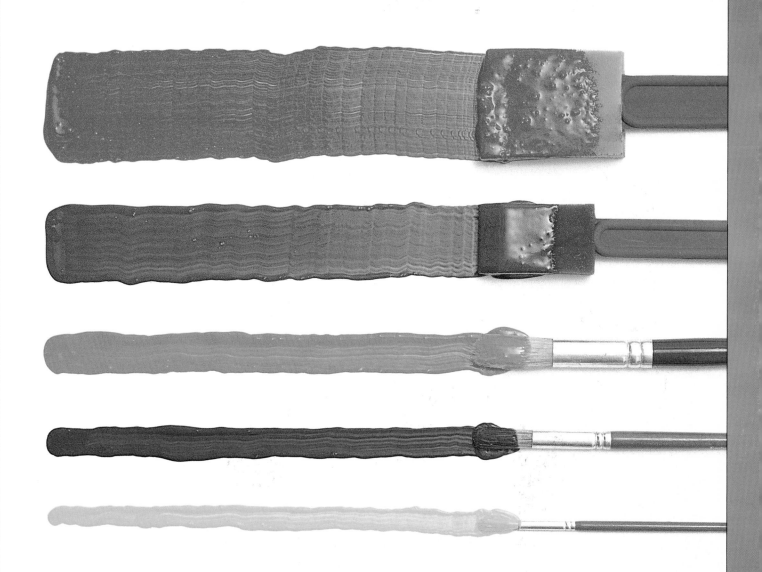

Which line is the narrowest?

Tom and Rose are building towers.
Rose has built the tallest.

Tall and Small

 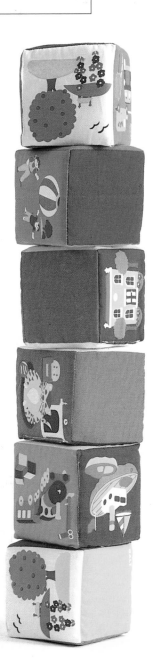

Which tower is the smallest?

Sam and Jack are playing with toy ducks. Jack's duck is a different size.

Same Size

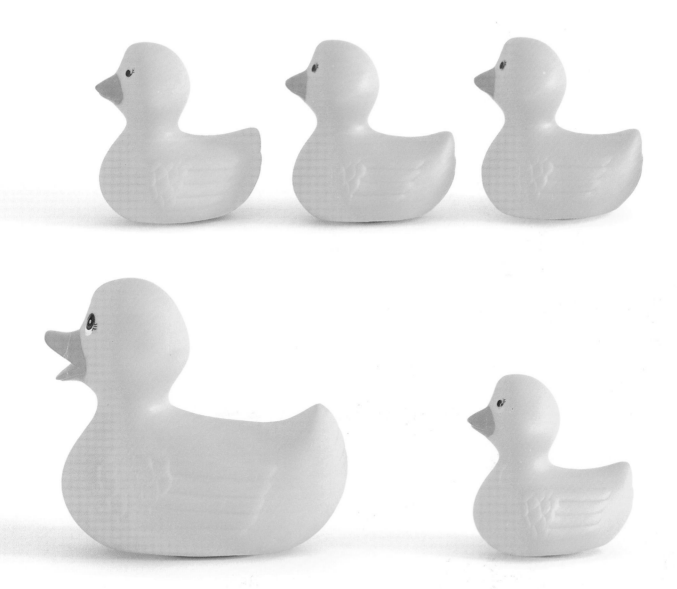

Which ducks are the same size?

People are different sizes too. Some are taller. Some are smaller. Some are the same size.

What size are you?